My Child
Miracle Beyond Words

by

Jennifer Leigh Mujica

Illustrations by Elena Wherry

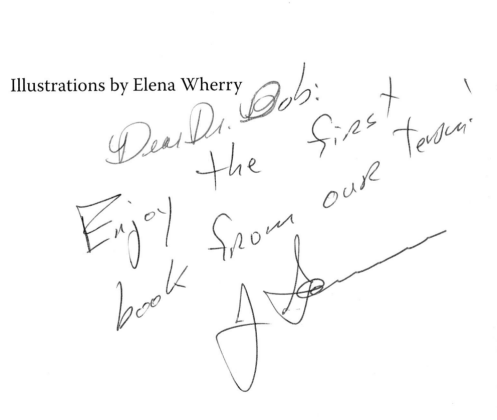

My Child Miracle Beyond Words

essi51@roadrunner.com

Original Cover Art by:
Elena Wherry

Book Design by:
Brittany Baum

Photography by:
Brandi McDermott Photography
www.brandimcdermott.com

ISBN 978-0-615-28920-5

First Edition: May 2009

To my earthly angels –
Sophia, Juliana and my husband, Gorge.

To my heavenly angel, my grandmother—
whose work ethic inspired me to finish this book
despite life's many responsibilities.

To each friend and loved one
that helped me stay focused
on making this dream a reality.

Dearest Reader,

A baby is pure beauty glistening with God's graceful love. Humanity at its most innocent stage evokes a sense of wonder about the miracle of creation. The abundant joy of a child's laughter has no equal, except the laughter of another child. Do you have time to appreciate these wonders? We are often too busy with life's day-to-day responsibilities to treasure these little miracles. My verses will reawaken a sense of wonder for both the blessings and challenges of life with children.

Beginning the journey of motherhood is embarking on an adventure into unknown territory. We really have no idea what lies ahead. The months before the baby arrives become a roller coaster ride of emotions – excitement, fear, anticipation and joy beyond measure. Then suddenly peace calms our hearts as we melt with love while gazing into the eyes of our beloved child. Within these pages you will travel along the first stages in the journey of parenthood through poems and verses that celebrate the miracles and challenges of pregnancy through the toddler years.

Who might you be? A parent, teacher, grandparent or childcare giver? Perhaps you just changed the fifth diaper in an hour and sat down for a quick break. On the brink of parenthood, you read these verses to get a glimpse of the adventures to come. Maybe you have no interest at all in motherhood but bought this book for a pregnant friend and decided to take a peek inside to see what all the hubbub is about (I won't be offended in the least if you slam it shut; we all have our own calling in life). The verses within my book are for anyone who appreciates the abundant joy of a child.

I share a special message for you as you begin reading. It's easy to understand why we celebrate wonderful moments with children. But why celebrate the challenges? As the years of my life pass, I begin to realize that the most challenging parts of life are, in the end, the most rewarding. Marriage, raising children, developing a career (finishing this book for heaven's sake!) are not simple. There isn't a short cut to a happy ending. But there is nothing more satisfying then looking back over the years of our lives and realizing we managed it all…and did a darn good job.

May this book be a sanctuary for you. Each poem is a gift – a quiet retreat in the midst of a busy day. Mothers will cherish these reflections about the treasured moments of motherhood. They are moments that pass far too quickly.

Yet many mothers struggle with parenting, especially in the first few months after childbirth. This book is also dedicated to you. Many of these poems were letters written to my child during my first pregnancy – a glorious time when all my dreams of becoming a mother came true. After my second child was born, I found myself in the grip of postpartum depression. The writing ceased. All beauty was gone. The "miracles" of motherhood became anguish and dread. For someone who always rejoiced in my role as a mother, I was in a place I never expected to be. Years later it became evident that stresses such as moving cross county within weeks of giving birth and my husband being deployed to war during my pregnancy were probably the triggers that set off this unfortunate condition. The precious love my daughter and I share and the great joy she brings me have made the challenges of those early months a faded memory.

It suddenly occurred to me that not all mothers are experiencing the miracles I speak of in this book. Their awareness of the beauty in their own child may be diminished by factors out of their own control. Perhaps you are working full time to support the family, busy with other children or suffering illness. I offer this gift of love to you. This book is a sanctuary where you can be reminded of the most special blessing in your life – your child.

Flower images will appear throughout the book when Elena Wherry's original watercolor paintings are not gracing the pages. Children remind me of flowers – each one beautiful in their own right. Yet each is so different. They need constant nurturing, love and care with the challenge of finding the type of care that works for their own unique personality. Do they need sun or shade? Is this a moment for gentle encouragement or firm discipline? No matter how many books are written – on both children and flowers – we find the answers only through our own trial and experience.

Whoever you may be – a mother, father, grandparent, teacher or a woman or man wishing to become a parent someday – these poems are my gift to you. The beauty of my own daughters inspired each of these verses. May these poems illuminate the beauty of every child in your life.

Most sincerely,

Jennifer

Soul of a Child

I hope to tell the magnificence of my child,
but my attempt is futile.
For no words can embody her nature.
And should my mind grasp words to explain
her beauty, love and innocence,
it would last but a second,
revealing only a glimpse of my child's essence –
impossible to capture with words.

My child's beauty is a feeling.
Her sweetness and joy a welling in the soul.
How to describe this great love
I feel for my heavenly creation?
My amazement at how a tiny cell
grew into my beloved child?
I say, in truth,
Divinity is living
and breathing
before me.

A nursery of love ready for you.
How grand the first moment will be!

Expectation

Sudden Change

Once a gentle breeze, the wind began to gust,
Churned by a force far greater than us all.
Tulips swayed to Earth as
Tree boughs fanned the sky overhead.
Old soil flew into a world of turbulence.

A change has come—
A change that means no turning back
and reaches to the center of a woman's soul.

A seedling – small and strong –
took flight in the Wind,
landing in a new place on Earth.
A place of miracles and dreams come true.
There the seed planted,
forever removed from its old world,
until nine months later
it blooms into a brilliant
celebration of life.

Are You Really There?

I am told you are here.
I cannot see you,
And I cannot feel you.
But I must believe the words
Of a doctor – a stranger.
This amazing creation of life
Gives no hint of existence.

Rest my fears, Oh Lord.
As I believe in my Creator,
Unseen to my eyes,
But alive in my heart.
So, too, will I believe in my unseen child,
Until he or she is big enough
To move and lend truth to a stranger's word—
Until I have you in my arms.

Grace

A way of life is gone forever.
Yet a new life filled with
Blessings beyond my wildest dreams
Shines before me like a rainbow.

When my child arrives,
these blessings will emerge,
slowly and peacefully
every day,
like a gentle spring rain
Upon my world.

The First Moment

As I wait gripped by anticipation
To hold you in my arms, dear child,
I wonder what beauty
my gift from heaven will behold.

The first moment I see you
What will your eyes look like
gazing up at me?
What color will they be?
What color is your hair?

For now you are a mystery
known only by rib kicks
and flutters of life deep within.
I wait to hold your tiny hands,
Whisper, "I love you" in your ear
and hold you always near.

Most of all, I wait for the moment
you are in Daddy's arms.
He has waited, perhaps more than I,
to hold you near,
for I always feel you with me.
He loves you, too, dear child.
Daddy longs to see you, smile and laugh with you.
We cannot wait to love you.
How grand the first moment will be!

In Waiting

Tiny clothes are folded with care.
New albums of empty pages wait for pictures of you.
Blessings from loved ones align our walls.
A home full of anticipation.
A nursery of love...ready for you.

Teddy bears are lonely
    waiting for baby's hugs.
Crib is ready, dresser is packed....
onesies, sleepers, outfits,
        tiny socks, knit hats, receiving blankets,
                hooded towels, little washcloths, shoes,
        more bibs than ever imagined.
For you, little one, this world is ready.

I wait for you to make the picture complete.
For nine long months our world
    has revolved around your coming.
Now I will soon hold you in our arms.
Free time will be a memory.
Tomorrow I will have only you.

The Miracle

Two hearts intertwine in love.
    Far, far away a new life is born.
Slowly, lovingly, the miracle of Creation begins.
Unknown to the lovers, life grows into life.
But God knows full well the gift that dwells within.
His heart gave the lovers love.
His Will brought creation into being.
From where there was once nothing,
    a Masterpiece unfolds.

A flicker of movement and Mama feels,
    for the very first time,
signs of her baby growing, moving,
a rosebud beginning to bloom.
Within her protective womb a blessed child will grow
until strong enough to face the world.
Months pass and delicate flickers turn into kicks.
    A tiny foot protrudes from her side.
Mama's belly rises and falls,
    seemingly not big enough for the child growing within.

A blessed moment…
Papa's strong hand gently rests upon her belly and
suddenly feels movement, too!
The first time feeling his child. His very own child.
Creation of our union.
No dreams here.
This is life – his child will be in his arms.

A new era of life has begun – parenthood.
Emotions swing between excitement and fear.
Papa knows, as Mama did, with the first flicker of movement
    that graced her soul,
a beautiful child has entered the world.
A miracle all their own.

Heaven bound my soul ascends.
My carriage ~ the wings of a child ~
my child.
A cherubim bringing joy
beyond all I knew before.

Welcome, Baby!

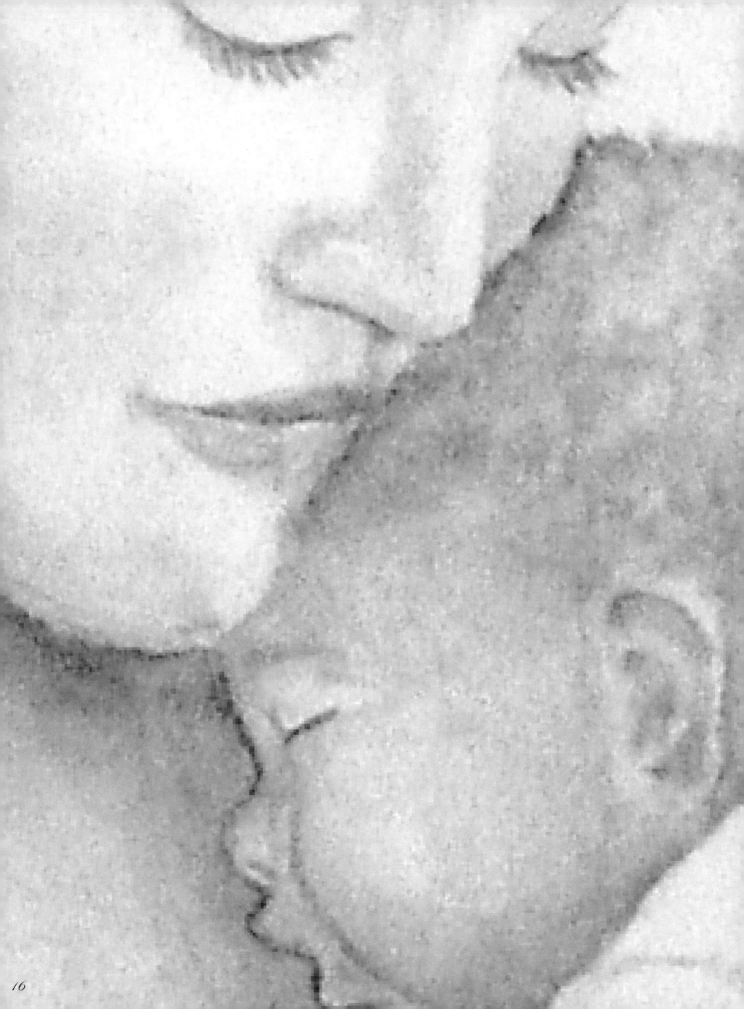

Divine Passage

Heaven bound my soul ascends.
Worries of today far below,
Meaningless specks in the Universe.

My carriage – the wings of a child – my Sophia.
So newly given unto this Earth from God's hand
Innocence illuminates my angelic baby.

A single touch takes me straight to God Himself.
Rocking, rocking, enveloping my angel in love.
My cradled arms are a passage to heaven.

You Are Here

Mommy sleeps in the mid-day light,
weary from a sleepless night
of waking cries and endless feedings.
A playful baby is by her side,
hundreds of miles from sleep.
Safe in the haven of Mommy's arms,
baby is wide awake – ready to play –
  nudging mommy from sleep.

A gentle touch tickles Mommy's cheek.
Tiny fingers wander over her nose, inside her lips,
firmly pinching as if Mommy were a toy.
Feathery touches tickle her face.
Eyes closed, blindness sharpens her senses.

Mommy ponders, "I'll never forget the days
when you were only a fluttering motion in my belly…
A distant heartbeat heard through doctors' machines."
Thinking to herself,
as disbelief rises within her soul,
"You are finally here!
My little baby, who was hidden for nine months
   is now touching, gazing, showing me love."

I open my eyes to see you.
Glistening eyes shine with love for me.
So many days I waited, empty arms longing to hold you.
Now you are here!
My child, you are all I've dreamed of,
all beauty, sweetness and love
wrapped up in this tiny gift from heaven—
A blessing from above.

Awestruck

Nothing made from the Creator's hand compares to a child.
Towering mountain peaks, grand canyons of golden splendor.
Double rainbows decorating the horizon.
Even sunrises of brilliant colors
transforming anew each day
do not match the beauty that I see in you.
Changes emerge each day, my sweet child.
The ocean may sound with mystery,
a hidden world of magnificent power.
But there is no match for the mystery –
The miracle of you.

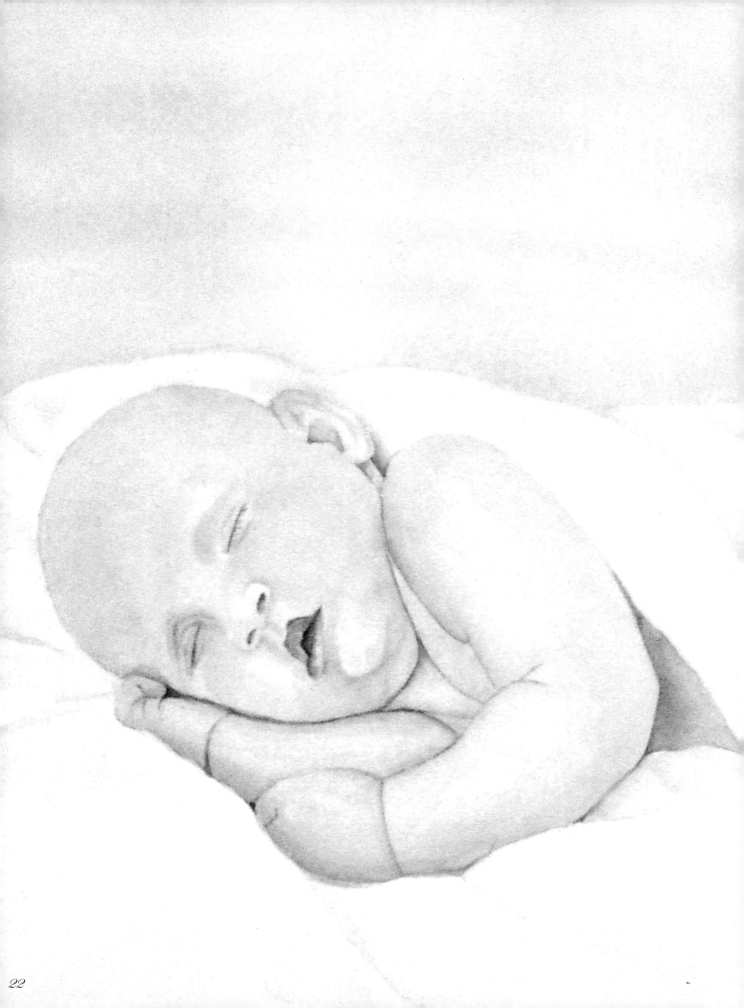

Rest Your Tiny Soul

Sleep, my child.
Rest your tiny soul.
For when you awaken
A big world waits
Full of wonders to behold.

Loud voices and smiling faces.
Bright toys – red, yellow, green and blue.
Soft kisses and loving whispers.
Tender moments just for you.

So rest your tiny soul, my child.
The world is a splendid place
Full of adventures all so new.
Hold tightly to my hand, dear child.
My love will guide you through.

Baby Days

Mama grows so weary
in the months since baby's birth.
Exhaustion like I never knew before,
rules my days.

Days are not mine—
    they are my baby's now.
Every minute is devoted to her care.

A portrait of angelic beauty...
My sweet child slumbers.
I get a moment to rest.

These first days are only a taste
of what is to come.
For slowly, gradually,
on the path of destiny,
begins a transformation far beyond my control.
A life that once evolved around
me disappears,
Replaced by the truest love ever known --
love of a mother for her child.

Love Blossoms

Each stage of parenthood
is a blessing
in the miracle of life.
As the Dawn wakes with mystery each morning,
what new glory will you bring my soul today?

Love greater than the Universe.
Patience to rival that of a Saint.
Openness to seeing beauty
in sleepless nights and inconsolable cries.
Parenthood constantly teaches the
Way to true happiness...
Love.

Baby Virtues

Joy

> in her giggles at simple things.

Love

> as constant as sunrise.

Beauty

> in eyes large with wonder,
> Baby's sweet face resting in my arms.

Devotion

> in her cries that ring out when I am away.

Determination

> to experience every inch of the world.

Hope

> for a new life.

Trust

> in my endless love.

Inconsolable Moments

What ails you little one?
Cries wail into the night.
When crying stops, bright eyes shine up at me…
Sleep is far, far away.

I changed the diaper, twice.
Your tummy is warm and full.
I rocked and sang you lullabies,
but yet you cry to me still.

Is this mysterious pain
known only in a baby's mind?
Perhaps, it's your new world
so scary, big and strange?

Nine months you were safe within,
my heartbeat a comfort from fear.
Now you look for me and listen,
but I am not always near.

I cannot be right next to you,
as I was for so long.
But I will make you a promise –
if I have to step away,
to you I will always return,
wrap you in warm kisses,
surrounding you in my love.

Mama always comes back.
During the moments I am away
Please remember...
My love is always with you.

Beatitudes for My Child

May peace always grace your world
  When the world around you is at war.
May harm never touch you.
 Though danger exists, may you, my child, be safe.
Hatred and greed may scheme to hurt you,
  But may only love fill your innocent soul.
When faced with illness, may you be strong.
  Upon adversity, may your heart take courage.

May Earth shine forth in grandeur before you
  So you may walk in Nature's beauty.
May you dance amid the flowers
  And sing in bright sunshine.
May your soul be filled with love and joy.
May harmony with all Creation bring you peace.

My Creation

While you sleep
boundless energy ceases.
Calm gives beauty
to soft eyes closed upon a gentle face.

While you sleep
I gaze with love
and realize the truth:
You are my child.

My creation.
Fruit of my womb.
A life given unto my care
forever.
Oh how I love you, my Child.

Sanctuary

My child's first years on Earth
are my only chance to build a sanctuary.
Villains -- hatred, jealousy and war --
    live far beyond the boundaries of my baby's world.
Baby ears do not understand war.
Baby eyes do not see racial inequality,
  wealth or poverty.
Evil is far away from our world.
    Expecting it will be a challenge to set aside society,
I can easily do so. Being with you is my ultimate joy.

Our tiny world will not last forever.
My shelter will be invaded.
The outside world will enter our peaceful life.
For now, I build with fervor and devotion
a home where you will grow and thrive.
A foundation of love
to give you strength as you grow older.

My gift to you – a sanctuary.
A place of happiness,
  giggles and cuddly love,
most of all –
Peace.

Working Mom

The dreaded day has come.
For the first time since you graced me with your presence,
I will be away from you.
A stranger will be entrusted with your life.
Neither Daddy nor I will give you care.

But I will think of you every second I am away.

Our family moved to a new city, shortly after your birth.
Friends and family far away;
my baby lives in a tiny world
of Daddy and me.

Our souls are one.
Wherever I am,
you are.

My heart breaks to be away from you.
I have shown you the world,
brought laughter to crying eyes,
given you all the love you need…
then more.

I will love you for eternity.

Will she care for you as I do?
Even if she tries, that is my hope.
My most precious part of life,
I won't be gone long.
When I return we'll laugh and play,
rock and sing as we always do.
Always remember, Mama will come home soon.

To Mommy and Daddy ~

Beauty is mine to behold
when strong arms lift me high with laughter.
Bright colors and smiling faces,
that I would not know without you.
Soft blankets warm my toes,
because you wrap me warm with care.
My tummy never aches with hunger.
You know I am hungry and feed me,
often before I even cry.

I move around rooms, through hallways and down stairs;
 Across grass, beneath treetops, under a blue sky.
Without you I would see nothing,
for you take me everywhere.

My wobbly legs step one by one,
because steady hands – your hands
    gently balance me.
I sleep peacefully in loving arms,
lullabies calming my soul.

Each moment of my life
I know that I am loved.
What would I do without you?
How silent my world would be.
        I learn to love,
            I learn to smile
From the smiles and love you give to me.
You are my whole world –
    dear Mommy and Daddy!

Reality

Sleeping in a tiny crib is a gift unto the world.
So simple it all seems.
A bed, a blanket and within a quiet baby lies.
    A baby is not simple!
A child has come – a life that is ours forever.
A baby girl will become a woman.
    A baby boy will become a man.
Through loving guidance each tiny child becomes
    an individual.

Lessons of living we teach them –

    Learning to laugh,
      Moving on after a cry,
        Embracing Earth's beauty,
          Smiling kindly to a friend,
          Choosing what is good,
           Letting go of all the bad,
         Getting up after a fall,
          Standing undaunted by fear,
        Letting hope be inspiration, and
    Giving love to those in need.

On days when life's goodness
Seems far, far away,
(I promise there will be a few)
May Faith be your companion.
 The Lord will guide you through.
These lessons I give you now, in the early years.
And my prayer is they'll stay with you, dear child,
as days pass into years,
And generations upon generations
Bring gifts of wisdom new life.

Always Here for You

Lightly as falling snow, eyelids close in slumber.
I hold you, my baby.
Cuddled safe and warm in my loving arms,
a loud noise startles you from sleep.
Eyes burst open, wide with fear.
"It's OK, little one, I'm here."

You see me – sleep returns to your soul.
I feel trust as your eyes meet mine.
Suddenly, awareness strikes my heart…
Your life is mine to guard and protect.
As I see the fear in your eyes
vanish into calm upon seeing me,
I know that from this day forward,
for the rest of my life, and the world hereafter,
I will seek to protect you, my child.

World of Love

My voice, my scent, my tightly cradled arms.
My heartbeat a soothing rhythm.
I am "home" to you.
I am your world.

Two people – Daddy and I – make up your tiny world.
You know only one feeling. Love.
From each inexplicable cry to moments of laughter,
hours of playing and quiet moments before slumber,
my child knows only love.

Union of Mother & Child

Softly, cheek to cheek,
We rock ourselves to sleep.
Resigned to exhaustion you lay
peaceful in my arms.
With each feathery breath of love,
my soul rises, winged with the innocence of a child,
to heavenly realms.
Reunited with God
by the union of Mother and Child.

To you, my child,
I grant Spirit of Wind.
To travel around the world
Without fear – limitless –
Inspired by Nature's energy
On journeys of the soul.

Toddler Years!

Heart and Spirit of a Child

Fascination!   Wonder!   Joy!   Determination!

Moments of frustration emerge
In shaky legs not ready to walk.
Silly tongue will not utter words.
But those moments pass,
And a spirit of enthusiasm rules!

Curiosity!   Love!   Joy!   Excitement!

A child's spirit invigorates all of us.
Grandparents dance again.
Parents giggle and run with youthful energy.
The joy of a child awakens the weariest souls.

When I watch my child's eyes
Sparkle with delight,
Joy grows within,
Bigger and bigger each day.

The spirit of a child
Joy and wonder
Replenishes our souls with vigor.

I pray our souls are united
In joy and love
All the years to come.

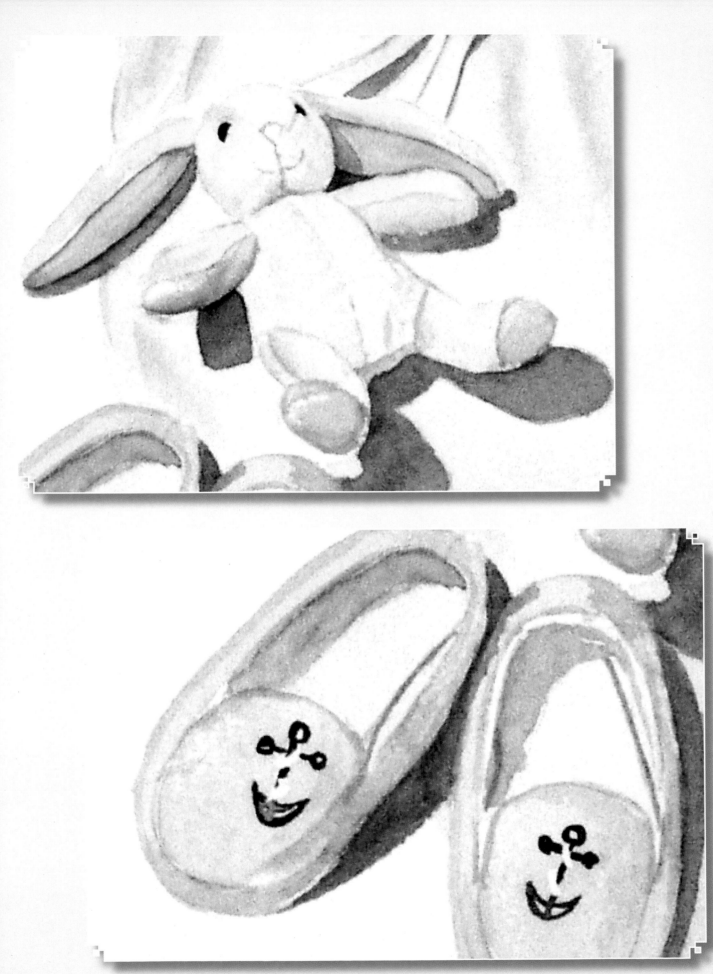

Detachment

Mama's arms dangle...empty
as a dusty bassinet
in an attic of childhood memories.
Not dusty so much as –
tiny feet dash quickly by –
    empty.

It was yesterday I held you,
a newborn life,
for hours both day and night.
Now a little girl runs where my
helpless newborn once laid.
My arms are no longer
 your pathway to the world.

I ask, do you still need me?

We share our life in grand new ways.
I am in constant wonder!
We dance and sing,
run together through the grass,
laugh about a cuddly bear Pooh
and animals at the zoo.

Yes. You still need me.

I show my child the little things—
   red flowers, green grass,
   ladybugs flying to blue sky.
A child explores,
but a parent teaches what they see.

My arms are not empty.
They are FREE!
Free to lead you
Into a lifelong
journey of adventure.

49

Discovery

New talents arise each day.
   How smart you are, little one!
A tiny person, so new to the world,
   reaches milestones at lightning speed.
Sweet one, your brain bustles with activity,
always wanting to touch, feel and explore the world.

Just as I get used to you rolling
   after being only able to lie on your back,
sitting up becomes a favorite habit.
I see steady concentration as you try
   to stay upright until balance is lost,
   and my wall of pillows comforts the fall.

One milestone conquered, my baby's sight
  is always on new horizons.
Striving and searching for more,
   suddenly you grab the crib sides and—Wham!
    She's pulled herself up to standing…
    "Look, Mama!" her big smile says,
    "I'm standing just like you!"

Slow down, my child, don't grow too fast.
Cherished moments I must treasure.
They will not last forever.
My angel progresses quickly,
  Ba Ba Ba (the origins of speech),
Banging toys together as drums,
  I join you, and we become a band.
Tapping on my computer keyboard imitating me:
    You are so amazing!

For A Moment
I Hold You Again

As rare as a summer day in the late months of autumn,
A moment occurs
When you want to be held for hours, close to my heart.
Feeling my love.
Embraced by my eternal devotion.
As a newborn sleeps in parents' arms all day,
You once again sleep upon my shoulder.
Never to let go.

Running feet do not stop often anymore.
Only a meal, craft project, a favorite movie or bedtime stories
Bring my little explorer to a halt.
Newly found strength and mobility are wings
With which you soar across the world.

Once content in our cozy home,
The great outdoors calls you to adventure.
Playmates bring you joy.
New places pique your interest.

So in this quiet moment when I have you again
In my arms,
I shower you with all my love,
Grateful for every second.

I ignore the phone ringing,
Shut my eyes to the clock that tells me dinner
Needs to be started.
All I do is hold you,
Giving you the love you need
In this moment of sanctuary for you and me.

Sharing the Wonder

My goal
is to enjoy life with the
zeal of a child.

You jump, my child,
Smiles bursting from ear to ear.
A scream with all the energy your small body can muster
Fills the air,
As if you jumped higher than a mountain.
Only I know that you left the ground barely an inch.
We scream and laugh with excitement.
You jump again and again and again,
Laughing with amazement at your feet's accomplishment.
Belly laughs get louder and louder.

Children are filled with such excitement about the world.
Why does it fade as the years pass?
Does youthful enthusiasm get smothered
By the responsibilities of adulthood?

A bug – the funniest object in my child's world.
Bug freezes in fear – then makes a dash.
My child stares at it – bug does not move.
She taps on the ground with her foot.
As soon as the bug dashes across the floor,
Scurrying then freezing again,
Every ounce of her being fills with laughter.
She stomps her feet, giggles endlessly.
Each scurry and freeze
Is a comedy show.

Simple joys.
Awesome wonders.
Beauty in everyday life.
Bring me zeal, Dear Lord.
The weight of many years lifts
When I laugh with my whole being…
Sharing in the wonders of a child's world.

Mommy Time Out

I adore you!
I love you, with all my heart!
My child, you are my joy and inspiration.
The meaning of my existence.
But please
please
GO TO SLEEP!

Hours have passed.
And you still squirm and call for me.
Every excuse to delay sleep
 Flies from your clever little mind:
"More juice!" "Go Potty!" "Read story again!"

I know (and you know) you have me hooked.
Manipulation is a toddler's inherent tool
For getting what he wants.

Just sleep, my baby, sleep!
I need a few moments of time
just for me,
please?

I'm It ~ Your Role Model

Babies learn to interact in the world
By watching the adults in their life.
If I cough, you cough after me.
I pat my chest,
pat, pat, pat, you do, too.
I play like a choo choo train.
Soon behind me is a little *chug a chug a chug a*

I smile, you smile.
I frown, you frown.
I laugh out loud,
You burst into laughter, too!

I often think…am I doing things right?
Am I a good example of how to live life?
There is so much to teach and show you.
Have I missed anything
That will make you a better person?

If I can show you Beauty
And happiness of heart,
Most of all, nurture a desire
To learn and love
I certainly have done one small part.

Your eyes smiling with admiration
Look up at me.
I am your guide through life.
I pray for strength and wisdom
To put forth my best for you each day.

Footsteps at Midnight

Midnight passed hours ago.
The house is silent.
My children are resting.
At this age
Sleep is the only time they are quiet,
Charging up energy to run again tomorrow.
I cherish the silence.

I begin to drift to sleep, when I hear
Tiny footsteps shuffle quickly to our bedroom.
Along the hallways lit by nightlights
Comes my two-year-old daughter – my baby—Juliana.

She wants to stay in bed with me these days.
Most nights I sigh in frustration
And lovingly lead her back to bed.
But tonight – awakened already –
I sense her needs more clearly.
She woke alone,
her room dark and silent.
The silence I cherished was scary to her.

Tonight I lift her in my arms,
Wrap her in warm blankets,
My arms surround her with love,
My baby and last child.
I hold you safe and warm
For as long as you want me to.
"Come with Mama," I whisper.
　　　　Her dark, scary room
　　　　　　will remain empty tonight.

Imagination

I am ready for our adventure
To magical kingdoms
Space walks on the moon
Across the Universe
On journeys in our living room.

A child's imagination is limitless.
Creativity beyond adult understanding.
Cardboard boxes are rockets.
Kitchen chairs -- a passenger train.
We chugga chugga all day!

I am a Fireman!
I am a Princess!
I am a Pilot!

My chairs and couches are filled
With dolls and animals ready for a journey.
Mission, ready! Here we go!
On a big jet plane ride.

Ocean stretches far below.
Galaxies of stars twinkle outside.
Prepare for landing!

My child says, "The limo is waiting."
"What is a limo?" Mama asks.
"I don't know…what is it?"
I smile at sweet innocence.
My heart is filled with love.

Big steps from couch to floor.
Now we are on a BOAT ride!
To a BBQ in Auntie's backyard in Ohio.
Back on the plane, seat belts fastened.
Captain pilots us home.
Home again in the playroom.

Thank you, Captain!
What far reaching lands will we explore tomorrow?
I am Pirate Princess, President of the United States!
Excitement awaits for sure!
Next stop – to the kitchen for a snack.

Spirit of Wind

Spirit of Wind
Climbs through forests
Soars across meadows
Meanders along river valleys
Rippling calm waters into torrents of foam.

To you, my child,
I grant Spirit of Wind.
Singing to heaven like a songbird.
Jumping in puddles
With laughter deep in the soul.
Climbing trees to reach
A mountain top's view.
Rolling down hills…giggling till you're blue.

To you, my child,
I grant Spirit of Wind.
To travel around the world
Without fear – limitless –
Inspired by Nature's energy
On journeys of discovery.

All I ask
Is for one brief, fleeting moment,
Stop and glance my way,
Love charms flying from your smile.
So that as my Spirit of Wind
Blows into years to come,
I can always remember you
As my child.

Did you enjoy reading this book?

Do you wish to read more poetry by Jennifer Mujica about children and parenthood?
Please send your thoughts and comments to the author by sending an email to:
MyChildMiracleBeyondWords@gmail.com.